180 Days
The Book Of Affirmations

BY HUGH WILLIAMS

Copyright © 2020 by Hugh Williams.

All rights reserved. No part of this book may be reproduced or transmitted in any form or by any means, electronic or mechanical, including photocopying, recording, or by any information storage and retrieval system, without permission in writing from the copyright owner.

This book was printed in the United States of America.

PREFACE

The inspiration for this book derived from me hitting one of the lowest points in my life over the span of one year. I became laid off, divorced, and financially inept all at the same time. The only thing that set my mind free to the road of resiliency was positive reinforcement. Much of the positivity came from changing my circle to reflect positive influences. My constant habit, every day, was to look for affirmations through people or periodicals. These affirmations, along with prayer, molded my darker days into brighter ones. Life is guaranteed to throw curves in life that we are not prepared for. The key, like every boxing match, is to get up and swing back. The unexpected problems of life can drain a person's soul. The right affirmations can be a battery to recharge our life and reset our day.

This book is designed to sprinkle hope into your life each and every day.

Welcome to a book of reinforcement. The book is 180 days of affirmations. May all whom read it find a journey to better days.

DAY 1
Turning Point

Within every tragedy there's an opportunity for growth. Every time that we fail is a chance to get up and see a new vantage point. Hitting rock bottom allows us to remember that there is a horizon. Our tears water our lives and allows us to grow into our life's lessons. Turning points in life are determined by our own interpretation.

DAY 2
TODAY

Today is a new day.

Eyes open... acknowledge the start of a new day.

Go to the bathroom...wash away remnants of yesterday. Today is a new day.

DAY 3
MIRRORS

Sometimes we have to stare into the mirror to see beyond our reflection. What we see is sometimes clouded not only by our interpreted physical flaws, but by the flaws of our past and the blemishes of our character. Embrace all that you see when you look into the mirror. There is perfection hidden in your imperfection.

DAY **4**
YOUR CIRCLE

Just because you may have people by your side does not mean that these people are on your side. To grow, the people you surround yourself with are very important. Your circle should have people you can learn and evolve from as well as reflectively contribute to. Often our growth can be stagnant when we surround ourselves with people who do not have similar aspirations. We become compromised when people we think celebrate us are actually envious. Some people have these traits because they wish they could do what you do, or they are not willing to put in the work. Surrounding ourselves with people who are greater or reflective of people we want to become is so very important.

DAY 5
PROBLEMS

Sometimes the greatest epidemic in our lives is constantly breathing life into our problems by constantly complaining. Instead we need to breathe life into our progress.

DAY **6**
CHALLENGES

Don't limit the challenges of life... instead challenge your limits.

DAY **7**
POSITIVITY

There is positivity in every day even if you have to squint to see it.

DAY 8
HARVEST

You cannot harvest the crop of a good life without planting positive seeds.

DAY 9
OVERTHINKING

Overthinking will cause you to do nothing. Sometimes it's just good to act.

DAY 10
PURPOSE

Live within your purpose and everything else will fall into place.

DAY 11
Comfort Zones

Comfort zones sometimes create dead potential. Routine does not create growth, just familiarity. Growth is like a muscle; it cannot grow without resistance and pain.

DAY **12**
Life vs. Diamonds

In life we are all into the pursuit of immediate perfection and gratification. We fail to realize that everything is a process. In many ways we can compare ourselves to diamonds. The diamond is the most sought-after stone for its luster, brilliance and beauty. When a diamond is in its raw state, though it is still beautiful, it shares common flaws and traits among other stones. The pressure of carbon makes diamonds. It is then molded, faceted and polished to create its brilliance. It is then centered around a shiny precious metal to make it shine even more. The moral of this is that there are going to be pressures in life that will make us stronger. Our experiences will mold and shape us. The right people we surround ourselves with will allow us to shine and be brilliant.

DAY **13**
8 Hours

In a day we only have 24 hours. Eight hours we spend working; eight hours we spend sleeping. This means that we only have eight hours every day to make our own shape to our own future. Make those hours count.

DAY **14**
MENTAL FOOD

Nourish your mind with positive energy and knowledge. Flee negative influences and gossip like the plague. It is your responsibility to keep your mind evolving, positive, and free. Remember, a negative mind cannot fulfill a positive life.

DAY 15
Recipe for P.E.R.S.E.V.E.R.A.N.C.E

Power
Energy
Resilience
Success
Evolution
Vibrancy
Enlightenment
Reverence
Achievement
Nurturing
Courage
Engagement

Take each of these elements into every facet of every day and you will persevere.

DAY **16**
THE 12 MONEY AND BUSINESS COMMANDMENTS

The measure of financial success lies in:

A. Living below your means.
B. Making money work for you.
C. Pursuing things you love and are passionate about.
D. Stop buying things with money that you don't have to impress people you don't like.
E. The only place where success comes before work is in the dictionary.
F. Never spend money before you have it.
G. The financial success comes from consistency.
H. People never buy for logical reasons; they buy for emotional ones.
I. Never be afraid to make mistakes.
J. Perseverance is everything.
    And finally,
K. If people like you, they will listen to you. They will do business with you.
L. Repeat all of the above.

DAY 17
BREAK YOUR ROUTINE

So much of our daily life is so predictable that sometimes we literally run on autopilot. Though, in the beginning, we master our day by creating a routine; that same routine is the death of our growth. Challenge yourself. Expose yourself to something new. It could be something as small as reading a different type of periodical or as major as taking an unplanned excursion. The process of participating in something new can plant a seed of knowledge and a different reference point. Never be afraid to evolve into a world that is always evolving.

DAY 18
DON'T LET DOUBT WIN

In life you are in a boxing match of doubt against your inner voice. Doubt is the bully that has stolen your potential and eaten all of your dreams. There are enough people and elements in the world that will say what it is you can't do. You do not need to let doubt add to that list. Take time to believe in yourself and listen to your inner voice.

DAY 19
SELF

The greatest journey you can take in life is a journey within. It is a journey to understanding self. We validate ourselves based on people's perceptions and not necessarily who we are. We are always taught to mimic and be reflective without taking the time to understand ourselves. There's power in being an individual. There's also power in being a free thinker. We are all born with unique qualities and traits. Why trade that to be like everybody else?

DAY 20
FAILURE IS NOT THE END

The road to success is paved with failure. There is not enough and not always an easy path to success. Sometimes roadblocks of life can come and build perseverance and wisdom in a situation. The building block is in trying. Failure is a teachable moment of your detour to a better road of life; not a roadblock leading to a dead end.

DAY **21**
GOALS

Life can sometimes make you deaf to the sound of your inner voice. Moments like these it is important to disengage, disconnect and reflect. Life's routines can sometimes derail us from our purpose. Create a vision board; look at it daily as a reminder of where you really want to go. Close your eyes and let your visions of your goals be your happy place. Take your time and chip at it daily. Speak, act, and think until you can grow into your goal.

DAY 22
ART

Life is like a canvas. If you don't pick up the brush of life and start to paint stroke lines with the colors of experience, you will never create your masterpiece.

DAY 23
REDEFINE THE IMPOSSIBLE

According to the laws of physics, a bumblebee is not supposed to be able to fly. The wings are too small to propel the bumblebee forward or upward; yet, contrary to science, the bumblebee not only flies, but is one of the most significant insects in nature responsible for pollination. The bumblebee defies science's theory of its flight being impossible to answer in defiance and say that, "I am possible."

DAY 24
LOVE IS BLIND

Love is blind because we many times see with our hearts instead of our minds. The eyes temporarily take a mental picture, yet at the same time the heart, at some point, takes over. We create a picture of the future potential, not taking time to see if the picture that our mind and our heart created is real. We never see if it is just a mirage of misdirection of a person's representative. There is no perfect recipe for love. There is, however, a chance to understand a person better if you make the investment of friendship. Taking the time to look beyond the attraction allows both parties to be free to exhibit their true selves and gives you a better green light to go further.

DAY 25
BE A LIGHT

The world can be a dark place, full of challenges and uncertainty. Let your smile be your window to your soul. Let your wisdom deafen the noise of rhetoric. Let your energy be the light at the end of someone's tunnel.

DAY 26
HAPPINESS

Happiness starts within a choice. It is not defined by a salary. Money can't quantify a level of comfort. It is not defined by acquired possessions. It is not even defined by a significant other. It is a journey within. The journey should be within the choice of finding things in everyday life that bring you joy. It is the willingness to reside in that emotion and incorporate that into the fiber of our lives. It is the willingness to live in a moment and navigate beyond the superficial means to celebrate our own life's purpose.

DAY 27
MEMORIES

It is our responsibility, or should I say it is the responsibility of us as humans to create good memories each and every day. Through life we acquire things and landmark accomplishments to build our hierarchy. The irony is that we forget that life is a journey and not a destination. It is full of dreams accomplished as well as dreams deferred. All are very significant in adding to our library of wisdom. Enjoy all of the lessons in the classroom of life, for, in the end, our memories will be the only thing that we have.

DAY 28
PAIN

Pain is sometimes necessary for growth. Unfortunately, we do not grow residing in our own comfort zones. Like muscles in our body, we do not evolve without resistance or, in other words, pain. Like our muscles, we get torn down, stretched and restructured. The consistent resistance creates a new strength. With this new strength, like a muscle, we can challenge our new obstacles of resistance. Over time, the pain sculpts and molds and defines the new version of who we are.

DAY **29**
Reciprocity

If you are a giver, it is crucial to your survival to align yourself with another giver and not necessarily a taker. Life is like two glasses of water, both a little bit more than halfway full. If you pour from each glass, as long as the two glasses are poured back and forth, neither will become empty. It is only when one glass is poured all the way into the other glass that the other one becomes empty. Life is about balance and you should seek those that pour into you just as much as you pour into them.

DAY 30
TEAMWORK

As the old saying goes, "teamwork makes the dream work." Without the moving parts of a car engine, a car is merely a standing piece of metal. Fabric is merely thread when it is a single strand. Without many, an army is merely just a soldier. The key to this and moral to this is that when great minds come together, brilliance appears. A feat would be impossible for one; but could be an easy path for many. It takes many parts, many people, and many minds to create something great.

DAY **31**
Opportunity

Sometimes the window of opportunity is rolling on four wheels and only allows you to look through it as it passes you by once.

DAY 32
WEALTH

Wealth is not birthed from having money; it is sustained by investing in a mindset married to opportunity and discipline.

DAY 33
BELIEVE IN BEING ENOUGH

Every time you wake up and look into the mirror, stare into your reflection and say these words to yourself: Say that you are smart enough; say that you are bold enough; say that you are kind enough; say that you are good enough to be enough.

DAY 34
WINDOW

Through every tragedy there is a window of opportunity.

DAY 35
AMBITION

Ambition can make dreams tangible. It can create the finish line of success. It can also create a pillar of sacrifice. It is the nucleus of goals and horizon of achievement.

DAY 36
NOW

Live in the now. Smell the roses. Grab the opportunity. Do not put off for tomorrow what may not come. Act on it today. So often we live with our dreams deferred. Often, we can only blame ourselves for goals blocked by temporary distractions. Living in the now can chip away at the goal, minute by minute. Our lives can travel a whole different journey by just acting within the now. Tomorrow is only a luxury that is fueled by the actions of today.

DAY **37**
MEDITATION

Close your eyes, block out the outside noise, introduce yourself to your inner thoughts, collect all of your emotions, release your pressures. Release them all through every breath that you take. Take a few moments a day to press your own reset button and then finally open your eyes to restart your day.

DAY 38
REINVENTION

It is said that we only use a small percentage of our brain power. If that is true, then this gives plenty of room to create our new patterns, new habits and new thoughts. It does not matter how or when we age, we still have an opportunity to learn something new. We still have the opportunity to learn something undiscovered within ourselves. We should not succumb to the automation of routine. Our lives should never be regulatory or predictable. Every day is an opportunity to figure out your own uniqueness through reinvention.

DAY **39**
Free Thinking?

Facts can sometimes be an endangered species. Many things in society are purposely designed to stimulate you to follow instead of lead. Everything told to you is not always true or gospel. It never hurts to receive information and dig deeper. Sometimes facts get lost in a field of maybes. It is important to read, research and use your own deductive reasoning to get to the place of original thought. Original thought is where you can create original perspective.

DAY **40**
Camera

Life is like a camera. You can frame it and set it to capture a moment. If the image you create is not desirable, you can delete it and start again.

DAY 41
"Rest…"

DAY 42
BLESSINGS

Sometimes the best blessings come when you are not looking, but always when it is badly needed.

DAY **43**
SUN AND THE MOON

Some people shine like the sun. Some people illuminate like the moon. It is always important to remember that both are just as relevant, and they can both get their chance to shine.

DAY 44
UPGRADE

Upgrade your life, the same way you would upgrade your phone or upgrade your computer. The world deserves the best version of you.

DAY 45
COMMUNICATION

You must decide when you speak with someone whether you are trying to vent or whether you are trying to communicate. Often our communication becomes arrested when one person lives within their own thoughts and leaves no room to be in receipt of new information. Sometimes our passions and convictions can deafen our ears to even having resolution. Communication is a reciprocal game of mental tennis that has no winner. It merely sharpens our game of life and understanding.

Day 46
Roads

Everyone's road is different. We are all the sum of our own experiences. Sometimes we envy someone's success, yet we do not know the road of how they got there or the road that they took to get there. We only see the end result. There are accomplishments and levels of success for everyone's road. We must be diligent in our own walk to travel on our own path. We can learn of detours from other people, yet we must stay on the course of our own destiny, of our own road, if we are to fulfill our own path.

DAY 47
CONSUMPTION

The way we need to grow depends on how we feed ourselves. We must nourish our bodies with proper nutrients. Our bodies are a temple not to be defiled by toxic foods or substances. Everything else in life is sustained in that same process. The people we surround ourselves with should nourish our experiences. Toxic people can block that path and narrow our vision. Our mind always needs to be fed with periodicals of knowledge and experiences of life and people. Toxic thoughts can block your blessings and arrest your development. In this sense, we must try to fortify all aspects of our lives because some things that we consume could poison us.

DAY 48
LAUGHTER

Challenge yourself to laugh every day. There is always humor in it, even if it's a bad situation.

DAY 49
TIMELINE

Never be so much a prisoner of your past that you cannot find freedom in defining your future.

DAY 50
CHANCE

Every day that you wake up is an opportunity to write out and carve out a new chapter of your life.

DAY 51
NOW

If now was a person, many would avoid him at all costs. Now is the gate keeper of our future goals. We shield the success of now by procrastination. It is easier to acclimate to a routine of everyday than to experience the newness of now. Now comes with a responsibility of action. It comes with a recognized urgency. Now makes us accountable for chipping away at a goal. Now allows destiny to lead beyond just a thought.

DAY 52
ENEMIES

The greatest enemy we have is ourselves. We predicate who we are through the lens of other people, not recognizing that the only thing we can determine are our own capabilities. We blame life or people for our failure instead of pointing the finger at ourselves in the mirror. Selfaccountability allows us to befriend our inner self.

DAY 53
Progress

Progress rarely resides in the comforts of your own comfort zone.

DAY 54
STRENGTH

Sometimes you never really understand how strong you are and how powerful you are until that is your only option.

DAY 55
PROCRASTINATION

Procrastination is like putting a movie on pause. You never develop the plot, or the story of your life, and you never see the goals or its true ending.

DAY 56
HUSTLE

Always remember that the word hustle is a word of action.

DAY **57**
LIVE

Live your life as if you are a reptile; shedding all the woes of yesterday like dead skin to present the new you of today.

DAY 58
CONTRAST IN THINKING

The same water that softens a boiled potato, can harden an egg. This theory proves that it is not always about the circumstance of a situation but what you are made of.

DAY 59
Transformation

We must divorce who we are to marry who we want to be.

DAY 60
SELFIDENTIFICATION

We misdirect so much of our focus on trying to find the right person that we forget that we need to become the right person.

DAY **61**
Attraction

The laws of attraction can make many capture our eyes, but only a special person can capture and captivate our hearts.

DAY **62**
Treatment

Never be a victim of being treated bad. Never be in a cycle of allowing others to make us feel less than who we are. Our actions and our tolerance teach people how to treat us.

DAY **63**
Forgive and Forget

Revise the idea of "forgive and forget." Learn to forget the details of what hurt you, but never forget the lesson and the details of what it taught you.

DAY 64
DEATH

The worst death is not always when a person dies; it is what dies in us while we still live.

DAY 65
COPING

Sorrow can be compared to an ocean. Many drown in it while others are forced to swim.

DAY 66
DECISIONS

The yin and yang of life is a balance of deciding when it is time to work harder and when it is time to walk away.

DAY **67**
LIVING

Many are alive, but do not live. Do not make a living; make a living out of your lifestyle.

DAY 68
Just Start

You do not have to be great to start, but you do have to start to be great.

DAY 69
RECALIBRATE

A poor mind can never create a rich life.

DAY **70**
Race

Life is a race in which your best days should never be behind you. A new finish line should be established daily.

DAY 71
RECOGNIZING

Once you identify your destination, you can begin to start walking into your destiny.

DAY 72
Vision Board

A dream is not an action until you give it tangibility. If you have goals in your life, create a chart and a timeline of all that you want. Put it where you will see it every day. This will cause you to create a light at the end of your own tunnel. This tunnel is toward your own goals. It also gives you a new sense of direction and purpose.

DAY 73
Character

Character and grace can take you further than money. The way that you carry yourself can speak for you without words. It can also shield you from any ill thoughts of many. Character can make people invest in you without conviction. Your character is your lifelong resume.

DAY 74
CLARITY

Clarity is a definitive to purpose. It is the epiphany that is the catalyst to action. It is the spark to many chain reactions. Clarity allows you not to question the what's. It defines the when's so you can see the why's.

DAY 75
LEADERSHIP

Never be upset when a sheep does not understand why you want to live as a shepherd. Both are necessary; but not necessarily equal.

DAY 76
Transformations and Transitions

Caterpillars are beautiful, yet their divine purpose is to go into a cocoon to become something much greater. As they go into the cocoon, after a certain time, they evolve into becoming a butterfly. Never be afraid to own your own transition. The end product can be just as beautiful as the beginning.

DAY 77
MINDSET

Hurt and truth are one letter away from being the same. Sometimes how we look at something determines its impact.

DAY 78
TRUTH

Truth is unapologetic about what is pretty or even about what is ugly, yet it is always pure. It is all three of these things at the same time. You can grow quicker from an ugly truth than a beautiful lie. Learn to always embrace the truth.

DAY 79
CIRCUMSTANCE

Circumstance can become your island, or it can become your sailboat. It all can be determined by your vantage point.

DAY 80
LOVE

Before you can have a healthy relationship with someone, it is important that you have a healthy relationship with yourself. Learn to fall in love with yourself first.

DAY **81**
Beautiful Life

It is not impossible to have a beautiful life. It starts with telling yourself that you deserve joy and then allowing yourself to accept it.

DAY 82
BELIEVE

Believe in your destiny to receive your true destiny.

DAY 83
Karma

A wise person never seeks revenge. They usually step aside and let karma do all of the dirty work.

DAY **84**
ACTION

Choose your actions wisely. Your future needs you, your past does not.

DAY 85
BEAUTY

Being attractive and being beautiful are two different things. How someone looks can attract many, but real beauty reverberates from within.

DAY 86
MEASURE OF A PERSON

The person who never makes mistakes is the person who has never truly tested their limits.

DAY **87**
Light

Being a light to the world is like being a flickering candle in the wind. So many forces will try to dim your light, yet you still shine.

DAY 88
TRUTH

Everybody has a story to tell; but few have their own truth to tell.

DAY **89**
Traveling in Life

You can't move your car of life forward if you stay focused on your rearview mirror.

DAY 90
LOVE

Life without love is like roses without petals or trees without fruit.

DAY 91
REVENGE

To all who minimize your self-worth or hate on you, success is the greatest revenge.

DAY 92
SIMPLE RULE OF LIFE

Use things, not people. Love people and not things.

DAY 93
VICTORY

Victories are synonymous with struggle. Even the brightest stars can never shine without the darkness.

DAY 94
FLY

Be careful who is around you when you are ready to fly. Some people may just be behind you to pluck your feathers.

DAY 95
Selfesteem

Selfesteem is the perfect vitamin for a healthy everyday life.

DAY 96
CONTRADICTION

Life sometimes reflects irony. The colors of the atmosphere of autumn are so beautiful yet it is the season that everything is dying.

DAY 97
HEART'S DESIRE

If a person really wants something, they will make time or find a way.

DAY 98
DOGS

When life treats you like a chihuahua, sometimes you have to show your fangs to show you're a pit bull.

DAY 99
Failed Relationships

A failed relationship is not a loss if, in the process, you have discovered and gained back yourself.

DAY 100
STRIVE

One should strive everyday toward happiness; not making your life a chaotic mess.

DAY **101**
GIFTS

You have been given too many gifts to just be ordinary.

DAY 102
Million

Love the person that makes you feel like the million dollars that you've never won.

DAY **103**
CONTROL

You do not have control over what someone does, or even what they say about you, you only have control over how you respond.

Day 104
Chapter

We all live different chapters of our lives. For that reason, you can never compare your chapter one to someone who is on chapter nine. There are different stories to be told in everyone's book.

DAY **105**
THE IMPORTANCE OF TRUST

Having no trust in life is like being in a vehicle with no gas. You can stay in it, but it will go nowhere.

DAY 106
The Importance of Wisdom

Being fearless, without wisdom, will make you a casualty.

DAY **107**
Hurt

Sometimes we hurt because of what matters to us, not always what is relevant to others.

DAY **108**
BRAILLE

In the game of love, emotions and feelings are always unseen. We all must learn to read braille. For love is blind.

DAY **109**
LIFE

Treat your life like a classroom, this way you give room to learn life's lessons.

DAY 110
Silence

Silence can be loud and powerful when everyone else makes the most noise.

DAY 111
BLESSINGS

When counting your blessings, always remember to count the people who poured into your life twice.

DAY 112
Laughter

Laughter is the language that connects all people.

DAY **113**
Rain

The rain can clean all and allow all things to grow or it can shield all and hide your tears and pain.

DAY 114
GETTING UP

Getting up should always be celebrated if all your experiences have been about falling down.

DAY 115
What is Synonymous?

Struggling is not necessarily synonymous with failing.

DAY 116
GPS

When you feel lost and life gives you struggle, ask God for his GPS to get directions.

DAY 117
Decisions

Permanent decisions should not be birthed from temporary emotions.

DAY 118
LISTEN

There is a lot of growth that can come from listening to people. It is important to learn to listen. We must learn to listen to people with our ears; we cannot hear with our mouths.

DAY 119
Vantage Point

Just because we see from different vantage points does not mean that we do not see the same object.

DAY 120
Oxygen

Communication is the oxygen that allows us to breathe in a relationship.

DAY 121
Peace and Understanding

Peace and understanding should always be friends; both are the passcodes to your freedom.

DAY 122
King and Queen

Nutrition and exercise are the king and queen that rule the kingdom of our bodies and our lives.

DAY **123**
Spiritual

There are many different interpretations of religion. Everybody's spiritual journey is a personal one. Though our roads may be different, the goal is still the same.

DAY **124**
PERCEPTION

Dig deeper than the surface of perception. Remember, when salt and sugar are poured out, they both look the same.

DAY **125**
Pictures

Sometimes the pictures that we create in our heads versus the picture that life has created are two different things.

DAY 126
REALITY

The realest thing that you can ever do is accept your reality. Once you accept it, try to find a way to create your own.

DAY **127**
TRUTH

People would rather consume many sweet lies than to ingest the bitter truth.

DAY 128
TRUE LOVE

True love gives an address to your heart and to your feelings.

DAY **129**
Fear

Don't let fear be the reaction that discourages you from making a decision.

DAY 130
TIME

Time is too short to waste on the trivial; it is too short to waste on the controversial; and it is way too beautiful not to enjoy the journey.

DAY 131
FEAR AND DOUBT

Fear and doubt have killed more dreams in your life than your willingness has.

DAY 132
TIMELINE

This minute should be the start of your hour to drive your productive day. Your productive days will be the gateway to a great month. Your great months will push toward an amazing year.

DAY **133**
Offering

Offer someone a happy piece of your heart, rather than an ugly piece of your mind.

DAY **134**
GOALS

Try to set goals that can excite you and scare you all at the same time.

DAY 135
Change

Change does not come by commentating on the sidelines; it comes by getting in the trenches.

DAY **136**
Winners

Winners are only losers who decided to keep trying.

DAY **137**
Clothing and Struggle

Struggle is the outfit that you wear today. You can try on the shirt of success tomorrow.

DAY **138**
Haters

Be leery of haters. People who have no life will always bring drama to yours.

DAY **139**
Reason for Hate and Envy (Dislike)

Sometimes people don't always dislike you because you are a bad person. Sometimes they dislike you because you are a template of what they want to be and who they want to become. These are the people that you should kill with your success and then bury them with your smile.

DAY 140
CONFIDENCE

Sometimes confidence is not in how many people like you, it is being okay with the ones that don't.

DAY **141**
Assessment

You can be quirky, nerdy, beautiful, flawed, and magical and still have room to be confident.

DAY 142
REAL LOVE

Real love strips you down to your core. It allows your feelings to be naked and your flaws to be signs in passing. It reminds you that your progress is a journey, not a destination. It means standing with someone when the skies are gray and not always when they are blue. It means allowing a person to be a mirror to the things that cannot be seen and for you to be the same for them. It means both being willing to create a uniqueness and a oneness to carve out a oneofakind life experience. Real love is not perfection, yet the journey can create many perfect moments.

DAY 143
CHANGE

Change changes the address to happiness in your life all of the time. For that reason, you should stop looking for happiness in the same place that you lost it.

DAY 144
PREPARATION

Saving money should be a preemptive measure. As the old saying once said, "you should never wait for rain for build an ark." The same principal applies to money. Money should be saved to offset the future unexpected struggles or in laymen's terms, "a rainy day."

DAY **145**
Abundance

Let abundance be your emotional oasis. Wealth is your island with trees bearing fruit of prosperity, accomplishments, and efforts. Wealth comes in many forms. All forms are linked together. It first starts spiritually with all the gifts the Creator put in you. Your confidence amplifies the possibilities of execution. The second is the health. Your health transcends from the thought to your actions. The maintenance of health maintains the highway to all of your energy and dreams. The latter is the actual physical abundance of monetary gain. Health, spirituality, physicality, and mindset all the foundation of abundance.

DAY 146
LIVE, LEARN, LOVE

Life teaches us the value of financial gain. Life teaches us to work harder, be better, hustle harder...

As crucial as this is, equal value should be put into living, learning, and loving. If we spend too much time chasing dollars, it is possible to compromise the quality of your life. You can miss little things that can add to unforgettable experiences. We must take time to anchor ourselves in learning. Learning will expand how we think and how we see the world. Learning can give a vantage point unblemished by routine and be a Segway to wisdom. Finally, time should be made to show love and receive love from others. People enter our timeline for only a certain window of time. It is our job to live in the moment and value our friendships, our family, and our loved ones. Live life to its fullest potential. Learn as if the world is a big classroom. Love as though you will see the ones you value for the last time.

DAY 147
LIFE

Life was not meant to be easier; it is meant for you to learn how to be better.

DAY **148**
Bridges

Learn how to build bridges, not burn them.

DAY **149**
Know Your Power

You do not always have the power to change people, but you do have the power to change yourself.

DAY **150**
Joy

Work on your inner self. It does not matter the level of your abundance. Without your inner joy, your happiness could be compared to a leaking crack in a full glass.

DAY 151
WHAT GOD GIVES

God woke you up this morning, it is up to you to do the rest.

DAY **152**
Being Grateful

Be grateful for all the small achievements. Many raindrops can fill a mighty ocean.

DAY **153**
Living Life

Live life. Love in life. Learn from life.

DAY 154
THE EXPERIENCES

Every experience we have in life is a thread to our existence; woven in time we create a beautiful tapestry of life.

DAY 155
LEGACY

Create a life that is a legacy. Do not just dwell in the being alive. Create an existence worth living.

DAY 156
Irony of a Rose

Life has thorns that create pain yet, like a rose, those thorns can never take away from the beauty.

DAY 157
BEWARE OF NEGATIVE PEOPLE

Negative people will incarcerate your development and stifle your mood.

DAY 158
POPULARITY

You do not have to be everyone's cup of tea, but you can still be a popular beverage.

DAY **159**
Challenge Your Mind

You can only go as far as your mind will allow.

DAY **160**
Challenge Your Fears

Fear will make a puddle seem like a mighty ocean.

DAY 161
SEEKING GOD

Seek God first and all, including blessings, will come after.

DAY **162**
Taking the Leap

Sometimes we must all be willing to adjust for life's blessings. Some of the most significant stories in the Bible highlighted people that God called upon to do great things when they were not necessarily prepared or even ready.

DAY 163
BE GREATER

Dare to be great. Live to be a legend.

DAY **164**
NO TITLE

It is always best to under promise and over deliver.

DAY 165
Inner Drive

Let your ambitions run you so hard that you don't feel your feet touch the ground.

DAY 166
EXTENDING FURTHER

No person can be great at all things. The ability to ask for help and to delegate can take you further than your greatest talent.

DAY 167
ICE BREAKER

A smile can be the biggest ice breaker in a tense room.

DAY 168
WHICH ONE ARE YOU?

There are people who play checkers; there are people who play chess; and there are people who invent the game.

DAY **169**
Actions

A good life comes with deeds, not words.

DAY 170
Mode of Motivation

Figure out what motivates you before you drown in what stagnates you.

DAY 171
GROWTH

When trying to grow, be comfortable with being uncomfortable.

DAY **172**
DEFINITION OF YOUR JOURNEY

Courage, in its true meaning, means to do something that frightens you. It is not easy to face our fears, yet our fears are obstacles that hinder our life. We must sometimes look at the challenges of our fears as throwaways to a better existence. Sometimes we just have to be willing to close our eyes and step through that doorway. We fear failure and unconsciously limit our life's experience.

DAY 173
PERCEPTION

A glass of water that is half full and a glass that is half empty are the same. It is the perception that creates the reality.

DAY **174**
WHY ASK WHY?

It is not your job to always understand your calling. It is your job to answer it.

DAY 175
Isolation

Isolation is a peace and a poison. It can be a place to reset and revamp or it can be a place to run away from the daily battles that we were meant to fight.

DAY 176
THE TRUTH AND COMFORTS OF TRANSPARENCY

Transparency may allow us to feel naked in our truth but it's also a light to see depths of who we are.

DAY **177**
The Purpose of Legacy

Our mission in life should be about purpose and legacy. We strive every day for finances or even acceptance but without digging deeper you will one day question your own existence. We all were meant and born unique. Our DNA amplifies a skill or purpose. We must work each day to edify that purpose. People are watching whether we want to pay attention or not. Our actions are emulated whether by our kids or by others that look into the window of our life. For this reason, our purpose and our legacy are tied together and must almost function in unison. We must create a legacy of who we are and anchor it to our purpose. Our life must be a thread sewn into the fabric of our loved ones to live beyond our existence. Our purpose and our legacy should be married in our everyday life.

DAY 178
YOUR DAILY CHALLENGE

Be stronger, wiser, and better than your excuses.

DAY **179**
The Mathematics of Life

We are the sum of our life's experiences. We cannot embrace the fruits of the good without experiencing and learning from the bad.

DAY **180**
The Question You Need To Ask Yourself

Do we leave our dreams and aspirations in our own mental showroom or do we finally decide to take life for a test drive?

DAY **181**
The Honorable Mention

Thank you for taking this journey for 180 days to start feeding your mind and changing your process. Sometimes all we need is a different vantage point to anchor our success. Feel free to take the time to reread all that may help you to positively fortify your existence. If you enjoyed this periodical, please look for my future installment of affirmations to be released in 2021 entitled "360". Thank you for your current and future support.

www.ingramcontent.com/pod-product-compliance
Lightning Source LLC
LaVergne TN
LVHW051558070426
835507LV00021B/2643